BLOOD SUGAR
FOOD TO SHARE

County Council

Libraries, books and more.........

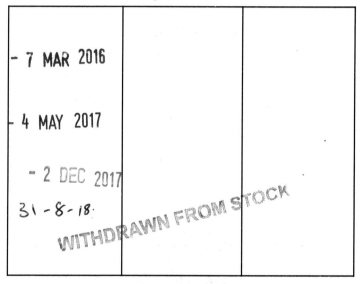

Please return/renew this item by the last date due.
Library items may also be renewed by phone on
030 33 33 1234 (24 hours) or via our website

www.cumbria.gov.uk/libraries

Cumbria Libraries

CLIC
Interactive Catalogue

Ask for a CLIC password

BLOOD SUGAR
FOOD TO SHARE

NEW
HOLLAND

MICHAEL MOORE

Introduction

From early and simple beginnings in the UK, Michael Moore started out in some of London's best restaurants, including the Cafe Royal and 45 Park Lane. Michael, whose love of food has inspired him to be on the world stage of international chefs who have a passion for great food and healthy living.

When Michael was diagnosed with diabetes, he was shocked. Having always led a fit, active and healthy lifestyle, Michael was more determined than ever to continue living his life as a diabetic without compromising on food.

After eight years of dealing with type 2 diabetes casually, Michael suffered a stroke and was forced to reevaluate how he was approaching food.

This is not a 'diet book', it is a collection of recipes developed over time to help keep diabetics, anyone who has suffered a stroke, or people who just want to eat good food while looking after your health, like Michael, on track without compromising on tasty foods.

Having diabetes can often complicate your plans when eating with friends and family. You are often left with the blandest of dishes and can be left at a loss for exciting dishes to try when eating out.

No longer does being a diabetic mean that you are stuck in a gastronomic wilderness. You can have great food that's unexpected and exciting. It's all about keeping your blood sugar under control and balancing the ingredients to help you maintain good health.

Blood Sugar – Food To Share is a great compilation of delicious dishes that will inspire you to serve and enjoy food again with your family and friends. The recipes are easy to follow and great for every diabetic who doesn't want to compromise on delicious food.

Recipes

Fresh Chilli Nut Mix

SERVES 6

180g (6oz) blanched
    almonds
180g (6oz) peanuts
180g (6oz) cashew nuts
1 long red chilli, seeds
    removed and sliced
1 long green chilli, seeds
    removed and sliced
1 teaspoon smoked paprika
    powder
drizzle of olive oil
sea salt and freshly ground
    black pepper
zest of 1 lemon

1. Preheat oven to 180°C (350°F).
2. Combine nuts, chillies, paprika and olive oil and mix well. Spread out onto a cooking sheet and roast in oven for 30 minutes or until golden and crisp. Turn out onto kitchen paper to absorb any excess oil.
3. Season with a pinch of sea salt, freshly ground black pepper and lemon zest. Serve immediately or store in an airtight container until required.

11

Full of flavor, this is a great snack.

Funky Mezze Platter: Roast Beetroot Dip

470g (1lb) medium-sized
   beetroot, washed and
   trimmed
1 tablespoon olive oil
½ bunch fresh thyme
1 tablespoon red wine
   vinegar
2 tablespoons low-fat natural
   yogurt
salt and pepper to taste
100g (3½oz) whole almonds

1. Preheat oven to 180°C (350°F).
2. Place beetroot bulbs into a roasting dish. Rub with olive oil and scatter over thyme leaves. Cover tightly with aluminum foil and roast in oven for 1 hour or until beetroot is soft. Remove and cool completely.
3. Peel and chop roasted beetroot. Place into a food processor with the remaining ingredients. Process until smooth and season to taste. Refrigerate until ready to serve.

Funky mezze platter: Parmesan chips

MAKES 12

230g (8oz) parmigiano
   reggiano (parmesan)
   cheese

1. Preheat oven to 180°C (350°F). Line a tray with baking paper.
2. Grate parmesan with a coarse grater. Place tablespoons of grated cheese onto the tray in 5cm (2-inch) circles, leaving enough space in between for each circle to spread. Continue with remaining cheese.
3. Bake for 2–3 minutes or until just melted and lacy. Remove and cool on tray until hardened. Store in an airtight container until ready to serve.

Funky Mezze Platter: Baba Ganoush

SERVES 6 AS PART OF A MEZZE PLATTER

3 medium eggplants
   (aubergines), halved
3 tablespoons extra virgin
   olive oil
1 clove of garlic
pinch of salt
2 tablespoons lemon juice
1 tablespoons tahini (sesame
   seed paste)
100g (3½oz) non-fat natural
   yogurt

1. Preheat oven to 200°C (400°F).
2. Brush eggplant with a little of the oil and rub each one
   with some garlic. Roast in oven for 40–45 minutes or until
   completely collapsed and soft.
3. When cool enough to handle, scrape out flesh and place into
   a food processor. Add remaining ingredients and process until
   smooth.
4. Taste and add more a little more salt or lemon juice if
   required. Refrigerate until ready to serve.

Funky Mezze Platter: White Bean Dip

SERVES 6 AS PART OF A MEZZE PLATTER

400g (14oz) cooked white
   beans
1 clove of garlic, chopped
1 bay leaf
2 tablespoons lemon juice
125ml (4fl oz) chicken stock
100g (3½oz) low-fat fetta
salt

1. Heat beans with garlic, bay leaf, lemon juice and stock in a
   saucepan for 10 minutes until soft. Strain and discard liquid.
   Cool a little before processing until completely smooth.
2. Add fetta and salt and process again until smooth.
3. Taste and add a little more salt or lemon juice if required.
   Refrigerate until ready to serve.

Smoked Salmon & Fresh Herb Mousse

SERVES 6

300g (10oz) cold smoked
   salmon
zest of 1 lemon
pinch of salt and white
   pepper
½ bunch dill, leaves picked
   and chopped
200ml (7fl oz) light cream
60g (2oz) butter, melted
½ bunch each of chervil,
   chives, parsley, finely
   chopped
toasted soy and linseed
   bread, to serve

1. Place salmon, zest, seasoning and dill into the bowl of a food processor and pulse until broken down, but not smooth.
2. Add cream and continue to pulse until salmon is creamy and smooth. Be careful not to overprocess.
3. Spoon into ramekins or dishes and top with melted butter and some mixed fresh herbs. Cover and refrigerate for at least one hour before serving.
4. Serve with toasted soy and linseed bread.

Chef's note: The melted butter acts as a natural 'lid' to preserve in the fridge. It can be scooped off before serving.

A great pre-dinner nibble.

Roasted Vegetable Salad & Lime Dressing

SERVES 6

2 small parsnips, peeled and
   halved
2 carrots, peeled and halved
470g (1lb) pumpkin, peeled
   and cut into wedges
470g (1lb) sweet potatoes,
   peeled and cut in thick
   slices
2 red capsicum (peppers),
   seeds removed and cut
   into thick strips
1 celeriac, peeled and cut
   into wedges
30ml (1fl oz) extra virgin
   olive oil
½ bunch flat parsley (or
   chervil, dill or chives)

DRESSING
2 tablespoons white wine
60ml (2fl oz) olive oil
juice of 1 lime
sea salt and freshly ground
   black pepper

1. Preheat oven to 200°C (400°F).
2. Toss vegetables with oil and season with salt and pepper.
   Place into a large roasting dish and bake for 40–45 minutes
   in oven. Remove and cool slightly. Toss through chopped
   herbs.
3. Whisk dressing ingredients together and season with salt and
   pepper; drizzle over salad and serve.

Chef's note: You can also include or substitute roast beetroot,
roast eggplant (aubergine) or roast onion.

19

Serve this at room temperature.

Shrimp & Cucumber Sliders

MAKES 4 SLIDERS

½ small Lebanese cucumber
sea salt and pepper
1 teaspoon olive oil
juice of ½ lemon
1 tablespoon natural yogurt
½ bunch fresh fennel tips
4 small seeded burger or
   brioche buns
8 large cooked shrimps/
   prawns, peeled and sliced

1. Using a mandolin slicer, thinly shred the cucumber into a small bowl. Season cucumber with sea salt and pepper, add the olive oil and a squeeze of lemon juice, leave to stand for 10 minutes to soften.
2. Stir together the yogurt and the picked fennel tips.
3. Drain any liquid from the cucumber and stir in the yogurt to coat it. Season with freshly ground pepper.
4. Slice open the dinner rolls and layer the cucumbers and sliced shrimp alternately on the buns. Pierce the centre of each roll with a small bamboo skewer and serve.

Light and fresh, these tasty little shrimp rolls are great fun for entertaining.

Sticky Pork Rib with Dip & Slider

SERVES 4

1 tablespoon olive oil
1 garlic clove, crushed
*1 teaspoon ground
coriander seeds*
*1 teaspoon ground fennel
seeds*
pinch dried chili flakes
*2 tablespoons light soy
sauce*
2 tablespoons agave nectar
*1 teaspoon English mustard
powder*
1 can crushed tomatoes
juice and zest of 1 lemon
*2 x 10 bone small pork rib
racks*
black pepper
*4 small seeded burger or
brioche buns*
1 small cob lettuce

1. In a small frying pan warm the olive oil and fry the crushed garlic for 1 minute until it starts to lightly color. Add spices, the dried chili flakes, the soy sauce and the agave, cook for a further minute. Add the mustard powder and the crushed tomatoes, then the lemon juice and zest. Set aside.

2. Preheat oven to 180°C (360°F). Place a sheet of aluminum foil into the bottom of a roasting tray and put a wire rack on top. Season the rib rack with freshly ground black pepper and brush with a little olive oil. Place the ribs into the oven for 45 minutes to begin cooking.

3. After 45 minutes spread a thick coating of the sauce over the top and bottom of the ribs, then return them to the oven. Continue to cook and repeat this glazing process 3 times more, approximately 10 minutes apart.

4. For the final glaze add all the sauce and turn the oven up to 200°C (400°F), to allow the ribs to color and become sticky. Remove from the oven and, using a small fork, pull some of the rib meat and place it between the lightly toasted buns. Top with the lettuce.

22

This is a light and fresh tasting sticky rib dish. The glaze can also be used for chicken, turkey or pork.

Seared Spice-Crusted Tuna Slider

MAKES 4 SLIDERS

pinch black sesame seeds
pinch white sesame seeds
½ teaspoon Sansho or
    Szechuan pepper
pinch ground ginger
pinch sweet paprika
sea salt and pepper
60g (2oz) Chinese
    cabbage/wombok, finely
    shredded
½ lemon juiced
1 teaspoon soy sauce
120g (4oz) fresh tuna fillet
½ teaspoon vegetable oil
½ teaspoon sesame oil
4 small seeded burger or
    brioche buns
1 tablespoon low-fat
    mayonnaise

1. In a small bowl mix together the sesame seeds and peppers with the ground ginger and sea salt.
2. In another bowl place the finely shredded Chinese cabbage, squeeze the lemon juice over it and add the soy sauce. Place aside to stand for 15 minutes until the cabbage has softened.
3. Meanwhile, cut the tuna into 2 pieces. Roll tuna in the spice mix, pressing gently to completely coat fish with all the spice mix.
4. Preheat a small non-stick frying pan, add the vegetable and sesame oil and sear the tuna on all sides for 30 seconds so that it is still very rare. Leave tuna to rest and cool.
5. Meanwhile, slice the buns in half and toast under a hot grill.
6. Slice tuna into ½cm (¼in) thick. Assemble the sliders by layering the tuna and cabbage mix as you like. Finish with a little light mayo to serve.

24

Using this recipe as a base, create your own sliders by adding chili, seaweed or pickled Japanese ginger.

Hot Smoked Salmon,
Potato, Lettuce & Dill Tip Salad

SERVES 4

2 slices soy and linseed
    bread
2 small chat potatoes
2 small cos lettuces
300g (12oz) hot smoked
    salmon fillet
½ bunch dill tips

DRESSING
½ bunch dill tips
120g (4oz) low-fat yogurt
1 tablespoon low-fat
    mayonnaise
zest and juice of 1 lime
sea salt and pepper
1 tablespoon olive oil

1. Cut the soy and linseed bread into small croutons and toast in a medium oven for 8 minutes until light brown and crisp. Allow to cool.
2. In a small bowl combine all the dressing ingredients together.
3. Cook the chat potatoes in salted water until soft and tender, keep warm.
4. Wash and trim the cos lettuce leaves then pat dry with a paper towel.
5. Prepare your serving bowls by arranging the salad leaves in them. Flake the salmon fillet over and cut the potatoes, sprinkle the croutons on the top and drizzle with the dressing.
6. Season and serve immediately.

Tip: Hot smoked salmon fillets are available at most good delis. It will look like it is already cooked, because it is.

I love this simple salad—it's crisp, light and really tasty with classic flavors.

Happy Family Salad (Swap with Tuna, Chicken or Shrimp)

SERVES 4

1 large head of broccoli
4 red radishes
1 small green courgette/
    zucchini
2 stalks celery
240g (8oz) three bean mix
4 eggs, medium-hard boiled
75g (4oz) fresh green peas
120g (4oz) feta cheese
1 red apple

DRESSING
juice and zest of 1 lemon
juice and zest of 1 lime
1 teaspoon Dijon mustard
60ml (2fl oz) extra virgin
    olive oil
sea salt and freshly ground
    black pepper
1 medium red/Spanish
    onion, finely diced
1 medium red chili, finely
    chopped
allow approximately 120g
    (4oz) of protein per
    person.

1. In a small bowl, whisk together the dressing ingredients.
2. Prepare a bowl of iced water and bring a large pot of salted water to the boil. Trim the broccoli into small florets and drop them into the boiling water for 1 minute only. Remove from boiling water with a slotted spoon and drop immediately into the iced water for a few minutes. Once cold, drain broccoli in a strainer. (You can use raw broccoli if you prefer the crunchy texture).
3. Using a mandolin, slice radishes, zucchini and celery as thinly as possible. Place into a large serving bowl. Drizzle over half of the dressing and leave to stand for 30 minutes.
4. Drain the three bean mix and rinse in a colander. Peel the eggs and slice into quarters. Add broccoli, bean mix and fresh peas to the serving bowl and stir together. If everyone is eating the same salad, add your selected protein or divide into bowls.
5. Crumble the feta cheese over the top, slice the apple and arrange with the wedges of boiled eggs around the bowl. Drizzle with remaining dressing, season with sea salt and pepper and serve immediately.

Lemon Chicken & Power Food Salad

SERVES 4

2 tablespoons agave nectar
1 tablespoon hoisin sauce
juice and grated zest of 1
    lemon
4 large chicken drumsticks
SALAD
80g (3oz) brown rice,
    cooked
80g (3oz) cannellini beans
2 scallions/green onions,
    finely sliced
60g (2oz) fried tofu, diced
2 tablespoons broad beans
2 tablespoons sunflower
    seeds
1 large ripe avocado
1 bunch baby cilantro/
    coriander leaves

1. In a small bowl mix together the agave nectar with the hoisin sauce and the lemon juice and zest. Place drumsticks in a large dish and brush with the mixture. Leave to marinate in the fridge for 2 hours or overnight.
2. Preheat a grill pan or barbecue and grill the drumsticks until cooked through and caramelised on the skin. Keep brushing this on as they cook. For a nice barbecue flavor, I even let the skin almost burn.
3. In a small bowl combine the salad vegetables and gently mix. Season with sea salt and pepper.
4. Mix the dressing ingredients into a small jar and shake well.
5. Serve the salad on the side with the hot sticky chicken and some lemon wedges.

I like to serve these together, but the chicken and salad both work as snacks on their own.

A Healthy Meal on a Pizza

SERVES 6

BASE

1 large pita or Lebanese bread
100ml Napolitana sauce
80g (3oz) button mushrooms, finely sliced
1 medium-sliced green courgette/ zucchini, finely sliced
2 eschallots/French shallots or red onions
120g (4oz) small bocconcini cheese
½ punnet grape or cherry tomatoes
½ bunch fresh parsley
90g (3oz) low-fat mozzarella cheese, grated

TOPPING

360g (13oz) baby spinach or arugula/rocket leaves
2 ripe avocados, diced
80g (3oz) low-fat feta cheese, crumbled
4 bacon rashers, grilled
½ punnet grape or cherry tomatoes
4 red radishes, finely sliced
3 tbsp fresh herbs
1 lemon
2 tablespoons olive oil

1. Preheat oven to 180°C (360°F) degrees. Place the bread on a large baking tray, spread a little of the Napolitana sauce over and then in a random fashion sprinkle the sliced mushrooms, zucchini and eschallots over the top. Chop the bocconcini, grape tomatoes and parsley and scatter them randomly over the bread. Sprinkle with the grated mozzarella and season with sea salt and pepper. Bake in the oven for 12 minutes.

2. Meanwhile, place the rocket leaves into a mixing bowl and mix with the remaining topping ingredients like a mixed salad, season well and dress with a little olive oil and squeeze of lemon.

3. Remove the hot bread from the oven and allow to cool for 2 minutes. Spoon the salad topping onto the bread. Cut into large wedges, season and serve

This dish can easily be changed to suit your taste. Simply add grilled chicken, sliced steak or grilled shrimp.

Quinoa Crusted Fishcakes

MAKES 8 LARGE OR 16 SMALL CAKES

300g (10oz) potatoes,
    peeled and diced
300g (10oz) fresh or canned
    tuna
1 red/Spanish onion, finely
    chopped
½ tablespoon fermented chili
    bean paste
1 medium red chili
2 eggs
½ bunch Italian flat parsley,
    chopped
2 tablespoons milk
sea salt and pepper
120g (4oz) white organic
    quinoa flakes
80g (3oz) flour
vegetable oil for frying

1. Cook the potatoes in boiling salted water until soft. Drain well and mash until smooth, then set aside to cool completely.

2. Drain the tuna, then place into a mixing bowl with the diced red onion, chili bean paste and fresh red chili. Add the cooled mashed potato, one egg and finally the chopped parsley, mix. Combine well and adjust the seasoning. The mixture should be firm and dry.

3. Divide the fishcake mixture into 8 pieces or 16 small balls and roll in your hands. Place them on a plate and refrigerate for 30 minutes to set.

4. To prepare for the coating, in a small bowl lightly whisk the remaining egg with the milk and season with a little sea salt and pepper. Place the quinoa flakes and flour into separate bowls.
Roll the fishcakes firstly in the flour to lightly coat them, then dip into the egg mixture and finally press into the quinoa flakes. Shape them into small patties and using a palette knife brush off any excess flakes.

5. Pan fry the fishcakes in hot vegetable oil for 2–3 minutes each side until crisp and golden, remove from oil and drain on paper towels.

Tip: Quinoa is a highly nutritious South American seed that can be substituted for most grains. It's available from health food stores and supermarkets.

The flaked quinoa creates a wonderful crisp crust which is much tastier and less oily than breadcrumbs.

Barbecued Whole Shrimp, Cilantro & Lime

SERVES 4

3 medium red chilies

1 clove garlic

1 tablespoon agave nectar

2 limes

12 large fresh shrimp (prawns) with shell on

1 lemon

300g (10oz) can of organic chickpeas (garbanzo beans)

3 tablespoons olive oil

1 teaspoon fish sauce

1 bunch fresh cilantro (coriander)

½ bunch scallions (spring onions), finely sliced

1. In a mortar and pestle, pound together the red chili and garlic to a rough paste, add agave nectar and the juice of both limes.

2. Preheat a barbecue or grill plate. Brush the shrimps with a little olive oil and place onto the barbecue to cook, with heads and shell on, for approximately 2 minutes each side. Allow them to char and turn a deep red. Meanwhile, cut the lemons in half and place, cut side down, onto the barbecue plate.

3. Drain and rinse the chickpeas in a colander, add to the dressing in the mortar and pestle with the remaining olive oil and the fish sauce. Stir to combine. Roughly chop the fresh coriander leaves and add half to the dressing with the sliced scallions.

4. Remove the prawns from the grill and arrange them while still hot onto a serving platter. Place grilled lemons on the side of the platter and spoon the dressing over the hot shrimp.

5. Sprinkle with the remaining cilantro leaves and serve.

Fresh, light and tasty, this is such a simple dish. Add extra chili to your own taste or replace shrimp with fresh grilled salmon or chicken.

Chicken, Grape, Pecan & Pear Waldorf Salad

SERVES 4

2 stalks celery
1 small cob lettuce, washed
  and drained
1 medium-sized roast chicken
80g (3oz) pecan nut halves
120g (4oz) seedless black
  grapes, sliced
1 ripe pear, thinly sliced
90g (3oz) seeded bread
  croutons

DRESSING
60g (2oz) low-fat
  mayonnaise
juice and zest of ½ lemon
60g (2oz) light sour cream

1. In a small bowl whisk together the dressing ingredients and chill in the fridge.
2. Finely slice the celery stalks, place slices into a bowl of iced water.
3. On a serving platter scatter the cob lettuce leaves. Remove chicken meat from the bone and break into small pieces. Arrange over salad leaves. Randomly scatter pecan nuts, sliced black grapes, sliced pear and the crisp celery slices over the chicken.
4. Finish with the croutons and drizzle dressing over the top.

Cold Set Chicken Pasta Salad

SERVES 4–6

1 medium-sized whole fresh
    chicken (I prefer organic)
1 onion
1 stalk celery
2 fresh bay leaves
8 black peppercorns
120g (4oz) wholemeal spiral
    or penne pasta
1 small jar of marinated
    artichokes (cut in quarters)
2 tablespoons whole
    almonds, finely chopped

DRESSING
2 tablespoons low-fat Greek
    style yogurt
2 tablespoons low-fat
    mayonnaise
zest and juice of 1 lemon
salt and pepper

1. Place the chicken into a large pot of salted water with the peeled onion, celery, bay leaves and peppercorns. Bring to the boil and simmer slowly for approximately 45 minutes.
2. Prepare a large bowl or pot (large enough for the whole chicken to fit into) full of iced water. Carefully remove the whole chicken from the pot and put it directly into the iced water and allow to cool completely.
3. Cook the pasta in salted water until al dente, and refresh under cold water. Allow to drain.
4. In a small bowl, mix the yogurt, low-fat mayonnaise and the zest and juice of one lemon. Season with salt and pepper.
5. Remove the skin from the chicken and pick the breast and leg meat from the frame, tearing in small pieces and placing into a bowl.
6. In a separate bowl, mix the pasta with the chicken and artichokes, sprinkle the almonds on the top and serve with the dressing on the side.

This method of cooking chicken creates the most flavorsome and moist cold chicken. It's ideal for any type of cold chicken dish, sandwich or salad.

Roasted Cauliflower
& Haloumi Salad with Sumac

SERVES 4

½ large cauliflower
200g (7oz) green beans
1 small can chickpeas
    (garbanzo beans)
1 knob butter
2 tablespoons olive oil
120g (4oz) haloumi cheese
1 tablespoon sumac spice
2 tablespoons sultanas
2 tablespoons pine nuts,
    lightly toasted
sea salt and pepper

1. Preheat oven to 200°C (400°F). Cut the cauliflower into small florets and place onto a baking dish. Trim the green beans and mix with the cauliflower, add the chickpeas.
2. In a small saucepan, warm the butter and olive oil together over a low heat, drizzle over cauliflower mixture and mix through. Place in a hot oven for 25 minutes.
3. Slice the haloumi into pieces and place onto a separate baking tray, spray with a little oil and bake in the oven until brown and caramelised. Remove the cauliflower, bean and chickpeas from the oven and dust generously with the sumac. Stir through the sultanas and pine nuts then season with salt and pepper.
4. Place the cheese on the plate and spoon warm salad on the top. Squeeze some lemon juice over the salad and serve.

Simple and easy but great fresh flavors. Haloumi is a versatile cheese and pairs well with asparagus. Serve with chicken breast or salmon.

Tataki of Salmon with Pomegranate, Citrus & Garden Herbs

SERVES 4

120g (4oz) fresh salmon fillet
1 teaspoon olive oil
½ pomegranate
60g (2oz) natural yogurt
juice and zest of 1 lemon
pepper and sea salt
selection of baby herbs
1 mandarin

1. Slice the salmon fillet as thinly as possible and lay onto a sheet of plastic wrap or greaseproof paper. Lightly rub with a little olive oil and lay another sheet of greaseproof paper on the top. Using a rolling pin or a clean bottle, roll the salmon fillet as thinly as possible and place into the fridge until required.
2. Remove the seeds from the pomegranate by half hitting the bottom of it with a wooden spoon and allowing the seeds to fall out into a bowl.
3. Whisk together the yogurt with a squeeze of lemon juice and a little of the zest.
4. To serve, remove salmon from the fridge and take off the top layer of paper. Rub salmon with remaining olive oil and season generously with pepper and a pinch of sea salt. Pinch the salmon between your fingers lightly and drop flesh randomly onto your serving plate.
5. Sprinkle the pomegranate seeds around and drizzle with yogurt dressing. Finish with herbs and mandarin segments.

Tataki means to flatten or hammer.

Sweet Chicken Skewers

SERVES 4

8 bamboo skewers
2 large chicken breasts
2 tablespoons agave nectar
3 tablespoons light soy
    sauce
juice and zest of one lemon
small knob of fresh ginger,
    grated
sesame seeds and fresh
    herbs, to serve

1. Soak the bamboo skewers in cold water for 30 minutes. Cut the chicken breast into small strips.
2. Combine all other ingredients in a small bowl. Thread the chicken strips onto the skewers and brush with the marinade mixture. Cook on a hot barbecue plate or in a non-stick frying pan. Don't keep turning but allow skewers to caramelise and even char on the edges, this should only take approximately 5–6 minutes to cook.
3. Sprinkle with some sesame seeds and fresh herbs.

Great for an outdoor barbecue, these skewers also work well as a quick snack or can be served cold in packed lunches.

Mini Fish Tacos with Soy, Avocado & Lime

MAKES 8 SMALL TACOS

120g (4oz) fresh kingfish
fillet, or other white fish
fillet
1 small scallion (shallots),
finely diced
1 small piece lemongrass,
finely chopped
1 medium red chili, finely
chopped
juice and zest of 1 lime
½ avocado
sea salt and pepper
1 small piece fresh ginger,
grated
½ teaspoon soy sauce
½ bunch fresh cilantro
(coriander) leaves
8 small crisp taco shells

1. Using a large knife, finely chop the kingfish and place into a small bowl with the scallions, lemongrass and chili.
2. Cut the lime in half. Cut one half into 4 wedges. Zest and juice the other half onto the kingfish.
3. In a separate bowl mash the avocado with a fork to a smooth paste and season with sea salt and pepper.
4. Add the ginger, soy sauce and half of the cilantro to the kingfish. Taste and adjust the seasoning.
5. To assemble, place small taco shells in a stand or between 2 small plates. Spoon in marinated kingfish mixture, top with a teaspoonful of avocado, scatter cilantro leaves over and serve.

48

Tacos are the perfect finger food for parties, and a great snack to have when you are watching a movie with the family.

Barbecued Salmon Sang Choy Bau

SERVES 4

2 teaspoons soy sauce

1 teaspoon agave nectar

2 salmon steaks

pinch ground ginger

1 tablespoon vegetable oil

½ bunch scallions/shallots,
  sliced

1 red pepper/capsicum,
  diced

2 tablespoons corn kernels

160g (5oz) brown rice,
  cooked

pinch dried chili flakes
  (optional)

200g (7oz) bean sprouts

pinch ground ginger

1 lemon

1 large lettuce (iceberg, cob
  or romaine)

1. In a small bowl mix together half of the soy sauce and agave nectar and brush over the salmon steaks. Dust them with the ground ginger and place in the fridge for at least 30 minutes or overnight.

2. Warm oil in a wok or large non-stick frying pan, sear the salmon steaks for 2 minutes each side and remove to a plate. After resting for a minute or two, use a fork to flake salmon into small pieces and set aside.

3. In the same hot wok, add the scallions, red pepper and corn kernels, then stir-fry together for 3 minutes. Add the rice, chili flakes if using, and a tablespoon of water. Add the salmon and any juices on the plate and stir-fry together for a one minute. It should be moist but not glugging together. Add bean sprouts. Add a squeeze of fresh lemon juice, season and serve in the leaves of cob, romaine or iceberg lettuce.

51

A great, shared family dish for everyone.

High Protein Spaghetti Bolognese

SERVES 4

3 tablespoons olive oil

8oz beef scotch fillet, diced
½cm (¼in)

240g (8oz) pork loin fillet
diced ½cm (¼in)

1 onion, chopped

1 garlic clove

a splash of red wine

120g (4oz) Roma tomatoes,
diced

1 punnet cherry tomatoes

1 can crushed tomatoes

600ml (1 pint) vegetable
stock

1 sprig of lemon thyme

120g (4oz) tofu, fried and
diced ½cm (¼in)

sea salt and black pepper

3 slices soy and linseed
bread

80g (30z) grated parmesan
cheese

240g (8oz) whole wheat or
gluten-free spaghetti

1. Preheat a large frypan or casserole dish, add half the olive oil and fry together the seasoned diced beef and pork loin, sauté for 3 minutes, then add the onions and garlic cook for another 2 minutes. Add a splash of red wine and reduce by half. Add the chopped Roma, cherry tomatoes and crushed tomatoes, with the vegetable stock.

2. Drop in the sprig of lemon thyme, cover with a lid and simmer for 45 minutes. Check that the meat is tender using a small knife, and add the diced tofu.

3. Adjust the seasoning with salt and pepper or add dried chili if you prefer, then reduce the sauce to a thick texture.

4. Toast the soy and linseed bread and put into a blender with the parmesan cheese. Pulse together for 1 minute to a coarse crumb. Add a tablespoon of olive oil, pour on to a baking tray and bake in a medium oven at 180°C (360°F) for 3 minutes.

5. Cook the spaghetti in boiling salted water as per packet directions, until al dente. Drain and place spaghetti in a large bowl in the middle of the table with the rich sauce on the top and sprinkle with the parmesan crumbs.

53

I always try to have a higher percentage of meat, but you can adjust to your liking or even make this with tofu.

Massive Meatball Bake

SERVES 4

MEATBALLS

175g (6oz) lean lamb or hamburger mince
175g (6oz) lean pork mince
1 onion, finely diced
2 tablespoon pine nuts, lightly toasted
1 clove garlic, crushed
80g (3oz) low-fat feta cheese, crumbled
2 tablespoons fresh basil leaves, shredded
2 tablespoons fresh parsley leaves,
    shredded
2 egg whites
30g (1oz) wholemeal breadcrumbs
½ teaspoon English mustard
1 teaspoon Worcestershire sauce
sea salt and pepper
pinch ground nutmeg
80g (30z) mozzarella cheese, grated

SAUCE

3 tablespoons olive oil
1 clove garlic, chopped
1 medium onion, diced
1 medium aubergine/eggplant, diced
1 green courgette/zucchini, diced
2 ripe tomatoes, diced
1 tablespoon white wine vinegar
sea salt and pepper

1. In a mixing bowl combine all of the ingredients together, except for the mozzarella, and mix well. Wet your hands in a bowl of cold water then, using your hands, roll the meatballs into 12 pieces the approximate size of a golf ball, then set aside.

2. Preheat an oven to 180°C (360°F). Brush the inside of a roasting dish with a little vegetable oil and place the meatballs into it. Bake in the oven for 20 minutes.

3. Remove meatballs from the oven and sprinkle with grated mozzarella cheese, and bake for a further 5 minutes to melt the cheese. Meanwhile, prepare your sauce.

4. In a non-stick frying pan, heat the olive oil and fry the garlic and onion together for 2 minutes. Then add the eggplant and zucchini and cook for 4 minutes until soft then add tomatoes and vinegar. Simmer for 10 minutes and season to taste. Spoon meatballs into bowls, spoon over sauce and serve.

55

Crunchy Chicken Nuggets

SERVES 4

500g (1lb) chicken breast,
   skin removed
355ml (12fl oz) buttermilk
80g (3oz) wholewheat flour
sea salt and pepper
pinch paprika
240g (8oz) raw buckwheat
120g (4oz) ground almond
355ml (12fl oz) vegetable or
   canola oil, for frying
Dipping sauce
175g (6oz) light sour cream
1 bunch fresh chives,
   chopped
juice and zest of 1 lemon

1. Dice the chicken breast into 3cm (1in) pieces and set aside in
   the fridge.
2. Pour buttermilk into a small shallow bowl. Place the flour into
   a separate small shallow bowl and season with sea salt and
   a pinch of paprika. Place the raw buckwheat into a mortar
   and pestle and grind lightly to just crack the kernels. Mix the
   ground buckwheat and almonds together and place onto a
   plate.
3. Coat the chicken in the flour, dip into the buttermilk and finally
   coat with buckwheat and almond mixture, making sure each
   piece is coated well. Roll gently between your palms. Place
   each crumbed nugget onto a tray lined with piece of baking
   parchment and chill in the fridge until ready to cook and serve.
4. Meanwhile, in a small bowl, combine the sour cream with the
   chopped fresh chives and the zest and lemon juice.
5. In a deep saucepan or deep fryer, heat the oil to 175°C
   (345°F) and carefully deep fry the nuggets, for approximately
   4 minutes. Remove from the oil onto a paper towel to drain.
   Serve hot with the sour cream dipping sauce.

I love deep fried chicken, and this lower
GI version is a fantastic alternative
to the fast food options. The buckwheat
absorbs less oil than traditional
breadcrumbs.

My 'Hot' Chicken Caesar Salad

SERVES 4-6

6 skinless chicken thigh fillets

8 low-fat bacon rashers

2 garlic bulbs

1 tablespoon extra virgin
olive oil

freshly ground black pepper

3 thick slices sourdough
bread

1 baby cos (romaine) lettuce,
washed

DRESSING

3 anchovies, chopped
(optional)

zest and juice of 1 lemon

¼ bunch parsley, finely
chopped, plus extra for
garnish

2 tablespoons extra virgin
olive oil

30g (1oz) light sour cream

2 hardboiled eggs, peeled
and coarsely chopped

30g (1oz) parmesan cheese,
grated

1. Preheat oven to 230°C (450°F).
2. Place chicken, bacon and garlic bulbs into a roasting dish.
   Drizzle over olive oil and season with black pepper. Roast
   in oven for 25 minutes. Rip up sourdough and add to the
   roasting dish. Cook for a further 15 minutes. Set aside to cool,
   then roughly chop cooked chicken and bacon.
3. Squeeze roasted garlic meat from the skin into a pestle and
   mortar. Pound anchovies, lemon and parsley until thick and
   smooth. Stir in oil, sour cream and eggs.
4. To serve, rip up lettuce and place into a bowl and top with
   chicken, bacon and toasted bread. Drizzle over dressing and
   parsley and sprinkle with parmesan.

High in protein, low in carbs, this salad
is perfect any time of day.

Summer Peach Salad

SERVES 4-6

4 ripe peaches, halved and
    stones removed
2 teaspoons low-fat spread
    or butter, melted
1 teaspoon caster (superfine)
    sugar

DRESSING
30g (1oz) low-fat crème
    fraiche
2 tablespoons unsweetened
    low-fat natural yogurt
juice of 1 lemon
¼ bunch mint, finely
    chopped
pinch sea salt
freshly ground black pepper
1 teaspoon agave syrup

SALAD
1 bunch rocket (arugula)
1 ball buffalo mozzarella
60g (2oz) pine nuts, toasted
½ pomegranate, seeds
    removed

1. Preheat oven to 200°C (400°F).
2. Place peaches cut side up into a roasting dish. Brush with a little melted butter and dust with sugar. Roast in oven for 25 minutes or until caramelised. Remove and cool slightly.
3. Mix dressing ingredients together and season with salt and pepper.
4. Place rocket onto a serving platter. Tear the peaches and mozzarella into pieces and scatter over the top. Season with freshly ground black pepper and sea salt.
5. Drizzle over dressing and scatter with pine nuts and pomegranate seeds.

This is my favourite salad.

Power Food Salad

SERVES 4

1 x 150g (5oz) can
   chickpeas
1 x 150g (5oz) can 3-bean
   mix
1 large red onion, finely
   diced
1 green apple
2 large celery sticks
2 carrots
juice and zest of ½ lemon
6 egg whites
1 cucumber, diced
150g (5oz) fresh podded
   peas
½ bunch dill, leaves picked
180g (6oz) hot smoked
   salmon, flaked
1 tablespoon each pumpkin
   and sunflower seeds
2 tablespoons olive oil
low-fat fetta cheese (optional)

1. Rinse and drain chickpeas and mixed beans. Place into a
   bowl with finely chopped red onion. Using a juicer, juice
   apple, 1 celery stick and 1 carrot. Mix with lemon juice and
   zest. Pour this juice over chickpea, bean and onion mix, cover
   and refrigerate overnight.
2. Lightly beat egg whites and pour into a large hot non-stick
   skillet (frying pan). Cook a few minutes each side, then turn
   the omelette out onto a board and roll up. Allow to cool and
   slice finely.
3. Drain the chickpeas and bean mixture. Place into a large
   bowl, retaining the liquid. Add 1 diced cucumber and 1 diced
   carrot with all remaining ingredients.
4. Whisk half of the reserved liquid with olive oil and drizzle over
   the salad to serve. Crumble fetta over the top if desired.

Chef's note: Hot smoked salmon is available in most good
   supermarkets and delicatessens. Alternatively, you can use
   fresh cooked salmon or trout.

*A fantastic source of protein! I often
add low-fat fetta to this salad.*

Scotch Beef Fillet
& Caramelised Onion Salad

SERVES 6

900g (2lb) beef scotch fillet
splash of extra virgin olive oil
sea salt and freshly ground
    black pepper
8 small pickling onions,
    peeled and halved

DRESSING
½ bunch parsley, chopped
2 cloves of garlic, crushed
2 shallots (eschallots), finely
    chopped
3 tablespoons red wine
    vinegar
2 tablespoons vegetable oil
1 bunch watercress, leaves
    picked

1. Preheat oven to 200°C (400°F).
2. Brush beef lightly with oil and season with salt and pepper. Seal on a preheated non-stick skillet until brown and caramelised on all sides.
3. Place into a roasting dish, along with onions, and roast for 45 minutes. Remove beef and rest for 20 minutes.
4. Return onions to oven and cook until completely soft and falling apart. Allow onions to cool and flake to separate the layers.
5. Mix dressing ingredients together and toss through onions, picked watercress and any pan juices.
6. Slice beef thinly and lay onto a serving platter. Top with onion and watercress salad and serve immediately.

Angela's Veggie Lasagne

SERVES 4

290g (10oz) pumpkin,
    peeled and sliced
6 large plum tomatoes,
    halved
1 tablespoon extra virgin
    olive oil
½ bunch thyme, leaves
    picked and chopped
cooking spray
12 dried lasagne sheets
210g (7oz) low-fat ricotta
210g (7oz) low-fat fetta
½ bunch sage, leaves picked
    and chopped

TO SERVE
zest of 1 lemon
2 tablespoons pumpkin
    seeds

1. Preheat oven to 180°C (350°F).
2. Place pumpkin and tomatoes into a roasting tray, sprinkle with thyme leaves and pepper, drizzle over oil. Roast in oven for 25–30 minutes, or until soft. Remove and cool slightly.
3. Grease a small lasagne dish and line the base with sheets of lasagne to fit. (You may need to break some in half.)
4. Spoon over half of the cooked pumpkin and tomato and crumble over a third of the ricotta, fetta and chopped herbs. Repeat with a second layer of lasagne sheets, pumpkin and tomato, cheese and herbs.
5. To finish, top lasagne with remaining pasta sheets and sprinkle over remaining cheese, herbs, lemon zest and pumpkin seeds. Roast in oven for 45–50 minutes. Serve with Spinach Salad.

Cut out the meat and cut down on the fat.

'One Pot' Chicken & Rice

SERVES 4

2 tablespoons olive oil
4 chicken Marylands, skin
    removed
salt and freshly ground black
    pepper
1 onion, sliced
2 cloves of garlic, crushed
2 celery sticks, sliced
1 red capsicum (pepper), cut
    into strips
1 yellow capsicum (pepper),
    cut into strips
1 x 425g (14½oz) can red
    kidney beans, drained
215g (7.5oz) brown rice
sprig of fresh thyme
720ml (24fl oz) chicken or
    vegetable stock

1. Preheat oven to 200°C (400°F).
2. Warm oil in a non-stick skillet (frying pan). Season chicken
   with salt and pepper and sear until golden brown, but not
   cooked through. Remove and set aside.
3. Add onion, garlic, celery and capsicum to the same pan and
   cook for 5 minutes. Tip into a large, deep roasting dish, along
   with beans and rice. Mix well and smooth out into an even
   layer.
4. Place chicken and thyme over the top of rice and pour in hot
   stock; cover with a lid or aluminum foil. Roast in oven for 25
   minutes.
5. Serve chicken on the bone with the rice or pull the chicken
   meat from the bone and mix through the rice.
6. Adjust the seasoning to taste.

Open Cannelloni with Pork Meatballs & Napolitana Sauce

SERVES 6

*485g (1lb 1oz) ground pork
   mince meat*
1 clove of garlic, crushed
*½ small red onion, finely
   chopped*
*1 teaspoon crushed black
   peppercorns*
sea salt
1 egg white
*350g (½lb) fresh egg
   lasagne sheets*
*300mls Napolitana sauce
   60g (2oz) grated
   parmesan*

NAPOLITANA SAUCE
2 tablespoons olive oil
1 onion finely diced
*1kg (2¼lb) ripe tomatoes,
   roughly chopped*
1 clove of garlic crushed
½ bunch basil, chopped
sea salt and pepper

1. Preheat moderate oven to 180°C (350°F). Mix ground meat with garlic, onion, black pepper, salt and egg white in a bowl. Dip your hands in cold water. Roll mixture into 14 even meatballs and set aside.
2. Grease a large baking dish and spoon Napolitana sauce on the base.
3. Trim lasagne sheets into squares and place a meatball into the centre of each one. Place into baking dish; repeat with remaining lasagne and meatballs.
4. Pour over remaining Napolitano sauce to cover and sprinkle with parmesan. Bake in oven for 45–50 minutes.

To make Napolitan sauce
1. Warm a saucepan and add the olive oil. Fry the chopped onion and garlic for 3 minutes until fragrant.
2. Add the chopped tomatoes and cook at a simmer for 45 minutes until thick.
3. Adjust seasoning with salt and pepper.
4. Before serving, stir in the basil leaves.

My twist on a lasagne.

Roasted Salmon & Baby Nicoise Salad

720g (24oz) salmon fillet,
   skin on and pin boned
splash of extra virgin olive oil
salt and pepper, to taste

DRESSING
1 teaspoon Dijon mustard
2 tablespoons sherry vinegar
90ml (3fl oz) extra virgin
   olive oil
1 egg white (optional)

SALAD
150g (5oz) small potatoes,
   cooked and halved
150g (5oz) baby green
   beans, cooked and chilled
130g (4oz) cherry or grape
   tomatoes, halved and
   roasted
60g (2oz) black olives
3 hard-boiled eggs, peeled
   and quartered
½ bunch basil, leaves picked

1. Preheat oven to 180°C (350°F).
2. Place salmon fillet, skin side down, onto a lined baking sheet. Brush with a little olive oil and season with salt and pepper. Bake for 7 minutes.
3. Meanwhile, whisk mustard, vinegar and oil together with egg white. Season and adjust consistency with water.
4. Place potatoes, green beans, tomatoes, olives and boiled eggs in a bowl with the basil leaves. Season and mix together.
5. To serve, spoon the salad onto the salmon fillet and drizzle with the dressing.

Impressive and healthy! Perfect!

Fennel Salt Swordfish & Ruby Grapefruit Salad

SERVES 4

FENNEL SALT

2 tablespoons sea salt

zest of 1 lemon

*½ bunch dill, leaves picked
    and chopped*

1 teaspoon fennel seeds

*4 x 180g (6oz) swordfish,
    tuna or kingfish fillets*

splash of extra virgin olive oil

SALAD

½ bunch celery

*1 large ruby grapefruit,
    peeled*

1 sprig dill or fennel tips

*2 tablespoons extra virgin
    olive oil*

1. Preheat oven to 180°C (350°F).
2. Pound salt, lemon zest, dill and fennel seeds in a mortar and pestle. Place mix onto a tray in oven for 15 minutes or until dried out. Cool slightly before pounding again to make a fine salt.
3. Brush fish with a little oil; sprinkle with the fennel salt.
4. Peel, trim and finely slice celery. Add some of the leaves from the celery heart and toss into a bowl. Segment grapefruit and add to celery with the juice. Add dill or fennel tips and mix; pour in remaining olive oil.
5. Sear swordfish on a hot barbeque grill for 1–2 minutes each side. Serve with salad.

75

I love this texture—crispy and fresh.

Warm Seafood & Quinoa Salad

SERVES 4

215g (7oz) quinoa
240g (8oz) sea bass fillet
240g (8oz) salmon fillet, skin off
240g (8oz) peeled medium raw
   prawns (shrimps)
150g (5oz) scallops
splash of extra virgin olive oil
salt and pepper

DRESSING
1 large clove of garlic, finely
   grated
2 sprigs rosemary, leaves picked
   and finely chopped
2–3 anchovy fillets, finely
   chopped
100ml (23/4fl oz) extra virgin
   olive oil
zest and juice of 1 lemon
salt and pepper

100g (3½oz) green beans,
   blanched and refreshed in
   cold water
1 x 25g (4oz) can of red kidney
   beans, rinsed and drained

1. Rinse quinoa several times in cold water and drain. Cook in a saucepan of boiling salted water for 15 minutes. Drain and rinse again. Set aside.
2. Place seafood onto a baking tray and brush with a little oil. Season with salt and pepper. Grill (broil) 4–8 minutes or until seafood is just cooked.
3. In a mortar and pestle, pound together garlic, rosemary and anchovy fillets until broken down. Add the oil, lemon zest and juice mix well and adjust the seasoning to taste.
4. Stir dressing into the quinoa, green and kidney beans. Spoon the salad over the warm seafood to serve.

77

Quinoa is a new supergrain which is high in protein.

Steamed Black Pepper Mussels

SERVES 4

1 tablespoon olive oil
2 cloves of garlic, finely
   chopped
1 bay leaf
1 medium green chilli, seeds
   removed and chopped
2 spring onions (scallions),
   sliced
freshly ground black pepper
900g (2lb) mussels, cleaned
splash of white wine
   (optional)
2 tablespoons light cream
1 bunch coriander (cilantro),
   leaves picked and roughly
   chopped
1 bunch parsley, leaves
   picked and roughly
   chopped

1. Heat oil in a large pan or wok and cook garlic, bay leaf chilli,
   spring onions and black pepper for a few minutes or until
   fragrant.
2. Add the mussels and a splash of white wine. Cover with lid
   and cook for 2 minutes. Shake pan and continue cooking until
   mussels open.
3. Stir through cream, coriander and parsley.
4. Serve hot from the pot immediately with some crusty seeded
   bread.

79

An easy meal or a starter to share.

Grilled Lamb with Pears, Pomegranate & Sumac

SERVES 4

1 teaspoon sumac spice

zest of 1 lemon

2 pears, cut in quarters

1 x 120g (4oz) can of vine leaves, drained and rinsed

1 cinnamon quill

1 piece of preserved lemon, rinsed and skin finely chopped

250g (8oz) non-fat natural yogurt

12 French-trimmed lamb cutlets

seeds from ½ pomegranate

1. Preheat oven to 150°C (300°F).
2. Rub a good pinch of sumac and lemon zest over pears. Wrap each in a vine leaf.
3. Place in a roasting dish with cinnamon quill and cook in oven for 45 minutes.
4. Mix together preserved lemon, yogurt and a little pinch of sumac; set aside.
5. Grill (broil) lamb cutlets for 2 minutes each side, or until cooked to your liking.
6. To serve, unwrap pears and discard cinnamon. Place onto plates with lamb cutlets.
7. Serve with a dollop of yogurt and sprinkle over pomegranate seeds.

Chef's note: French-trimmed bones are scraped clean. Ask your butcher to prepare them or you can do it yourself with a sharp knife.

Green Roast Herb & Lemon Chicken

SERVES 4-6

1 x 1kg (2¼lb) fresh chicken
1 bunch fresh parsley
1 lemon juice and zest
2 tablespoons capers
2 anchovies
100 ml (3fl oz) olive oil
sea salt and pepper

1. Place all ingredients except chicken into a blender and pulse to a paste.
2. Put the chicken into a baking dish, season with salt and pepper and rub the green paste well into the chicken, on and under the skin. Refrigerate and leave for 1 hour.
3. Preheat oven to 180°C (360°F).
4. Roast in oven for 50 minutes until cooked.
5. Remove and carve into portions. Serve with vegetables or salad, or allow to cool for cold sandwiches.

Chef's note: You can remove the skin on the plate and the flavors remain in the chicken.

Crispy Buttermilk & Nut Chicken Maryland

SERVES 4–6

625ml (16fl oz) buttermilk
2 teaspoons garlic powder
pinch of cayenne pepper
1 teaspoon paprika
pinch of ground white
   pepper
1 teaspoon ground coriander
   seeds
4 chicken Maryland pieces,
   skin removed
60g (2oz) dried panko
   breadcrumbs
30g (1oz) almond meal
cooking spray
fresh lemon, to serve
reduced fat mayonnaise, to
   serve
salad leaves, to serve

1. Mix buttermilk, garlic powder, cayenne, paprika and pepper with coriander seeds. Pour over chicken. Cover and marinate overnight.
2. Preheat oven to 200°C (400°F).
3. Combine panko crumbs with almond meal and mix well.
4. Coat drained chicken evenly in the crumb mix and place onto a lined flat baking sheet. Spray lightly with cooking spray and bake in oven for 50–60 minutes, turning chicken over halfway through the cooking time. Chicken should be cooked through with a golden and crisp crumb. Season with sea salt.
5. Serve hot with fresh lemon, reduced fat mayo and salad leaves.

Chef's note: Panko breadcrumbs are Japanese-style crumbs and are lighter. They can be substituted with conventional breadcrumbs.

Slow Cooked Turkey with Ricotta & Spinach

SERVES 6–8

120g (4oz) spinach leaves
180g (6oz) low-fat ricotta
1 clove of garlic, crushed
salt and pepper
1 tablespoon olive oil
3kg (10lb) whole turkey
juice and zest of 1 lemon

1. Preheat oven to 150°C (300°F).
2. Blanch spinach in boiling salted water for 1 minute and refresh under cold water. Squeeze as dry as possible. Roughly chop spinach.
3. Mix ricotta in a bowl until smooth. Add the spinach, lemon juice and zest, garlic and season with salt and pepper.
4. Force your fingers between the skin and breast meat. Spoon the ricotta mix into this area, spreading out evenly. Rub the turkey with a little olive oil.
5. Roast in a deep roasting pan in oven for 2 hours Remove and rest for 15 minutes in a warm place before carving.
6. Serve sliced turkey with roasted vegetable salad.

Keeps the top breast meat nice and moist!

Crusted Beef with Sticky Sweet Potato & Mustard Cream

SERVES 6

STICKY SWEET POTATO
700g (1lb 9oz) sweet potato
1 tablespoon agave syrup
2 tablespoons light soy
sauce

BEEF
480g (16oz) beef tenderloin
cooking spray
90g (3oz) sunflower seeds
90g (3oz) whole almonds
90g (3oz) walnuts
60g (2oz) low-fat spread or
butter

MUSTARD AND
HORSERADISH CREAM
2 tablespoons horseradish
puree or sauce
2 tablespoons wholegrain
mustard
1 clove of garlic, crushed
1 shallot, finely chopped
¼ bunch parsley, chopped
90g (3oz) light sour cream
sea salt and freshly ground
black pepper

1. Preheat oven to 200°C (400°F).
2. Peel and cut sweet potato into large chunks. Coat well with agave and soy sauce and place onto a shallow baking sheet. Roast in oven for 35 minutes, turning over halfway through the cooking time.
3. Spray tenderloin with cooking spray and seal evenly in a hot non-stick skillet (frying pan) for 2 minutes each side, or until brown. Remove and cool.
4. Process seeds and nuts to a coarse crumb. Add butter and process until just mixed through. Press nut crust onto beef tenderloin and reduce heat to a moderate oven 180°C (350°F) and bake for 25 minutes. Set aside to rest for 10 minutes before slicing.
5. Mix mustard and horseradish ingredients together and season to taste.
6. Serve sliced beef with sweet potato and mustard and horseradish cream.

One of my favourite Sunday lunches.

Baked Orange & Peanut Delicious

SERVES 6

2 oranges

2 egg yolks

60g (2oz) caster (superfine) sugar

120g (4oz) non-fat dry milk powder

2 tablespoons self-raising flour

120g (4oz) peanuts, ground

4 egg whites

cooking spray

1. Preheat oven to 180°C (350°F).
2. Zest oranges and squeeze 180ml (6fl oz) of juice from the flesh. Mix zest and juice with egg yolks, ¼ cup water, half the sugar, milk powder, flour and peanuts until well combined.
3. In a separate bowl, whisk egg whites until soft peaks form. Add remaining sugar and continue whisking until thick and glossy. Fold egg whites into orange juice mixture.
4. Pour into a baking dish of approximately 1 litre (2 pints) capacity, greased with cooking spray. Place into a larger roasting pan and pour in enough hot water to come halfway up the sides of the dish. Bake for 35–40 minutes.
5. Sprinkle with a little icing sugar and serve immediately.

Baked Chocolate & Orange Pudding

SERVES 6

600ml (20fl oz) low-fat milk

zest of 1 orange

1 teaspoon vanilla extract

90g (3oz) agave syrup

2 tablespoons cocoa
   powder, sifted

2 eggs

2 tablespoons butter

3 thick slices seeded brown
   bread

cocoa and icing sugar, for
   dusting

sugar-free ice cream, to serve

1. Preheat oven to 180°C (350°F).
2. Bring milk to the boil in a saucepan with orange zest, vanilla and agave syrup. Remove from heat and cool slightly.
3. Mix cocoa to a paste in a cup with a spoon of cold milk, then whisk into the hot milk. Lightly whisk the eggs in a bowl. Pour the hot milk mixture over the top (ensure the milk is not boiling). Continue to stir.
4. Spread butter onto the slices of bread and arrange in a small baking dish. Pour the chocolate custard mixture evenly over the top. Allow to stand for 15 minutes to allow bread to absorb custard.
5. Bake in oven for 35 minutes. Dust with a little cocoa and icing sugar. Serve warm with some light or sugar-free ice cream.

93

This is really quick to make. Everyone loves this one!

Baked Choc 'n' Nut Ricotta Cheesecakes

SERVES 6–8

NUT BASE
40g (1.5oz) chopped walnuts
40g (1.5oz) slivered almonds
40g (1.5oz) chopped hazelnuts
80g (3oz) almond meal
1 tablespoon melted butter
1 tablespoon agave syrup
1 egg white, lightly beaten

FILLING
900g (2lb) low-fat ricotta cheese
125g (4oz) non-fat natural yogurt
60g (2oz) agave syrup
zest of 1 lemon
2 tablespoons cornflour
2 eggs, lightly beaten
115g (4oz) very dark chocolate buttons
icing sugar and berries

1. Preheat oven to 150°C (300°F).
2. Process nuts in a food processor until they have the texture of breadcrumbs. Melt butter with agave syrup and pour into nut mix. Add egg white and mix well with a spoon.
3. Line the base of 6 greased 6-cm (2-inch) rings with greaseproof paper. Spoon in and bake the nutbase in oven for 15 minutes. Remove and allow to cool in the tins.
4. Beat ricotta in a bowl with electric beaters until smooth. Stir in yogurt, agave syrup, lemon, cornflour and eggs. Beat until completely mixed.
5. Fold through chocolate buttons and pour into prepared tins. Increase heat to 180°C (350°F) and bake for 20 minutes.
6. Remove from the oven and allow to cool. Remove from the tins and place onto serving platter.
7. Dust with a little icing sugar. Serve sliced with fresh berries.

95

Poached Pears in a Bag With Nut & Seed Crunch Cookies

SERVES 4

NUT AND SEED CRUNCH COOKIES

85g (3oz) almonds, chopped

85g (3oz) walnuts, chopped

85g (3oz) LSA (linseeds, sunflower seeds and almonds)

2 tablespoons sunflower seeds

2 tablespoons honey, warmed

2 egg whites, beaten

POACHED PEARS

625ml (20fl oz) pear juice or concentrate

120g (4oz) agave syrup

1 vanilla bean, split into four

4 pears, peeled and cored

1 lemon zest

sugar-free ice cream, to serve

1. Preheat oven to 180°C (350°F).
2. Place nuts in food processor and pulse until broken down into a rough crumb. Add LSA and sunflower seeds. Stir in honey and eggs and mix well.
3. Place teaspoon-sized mounds onto a greased tray. Bake for 20 minutes or until golden. Allow to cool on a wire rack.
4. In a saucepan, heat pear juice, agave syrup and vanilla bean. Drop in the pears and cover with a lid. Simmer on low heat for 20 minutes or until pears are soft and cooked. Carefully remove from the liquid.
5. Cut 4 large squares of parchment paper and place a pear into the centre of each one. Add a piece of the vanilla bean and a tablespoonful of the liquid with a slice of lemon zest. Enclose and seal by tying with twine. Bake in a moderate 180°C (350°F) oven for 12 minutes.
6. To serve, place the bags on each plate with a little of the pear cooking liquid on the side and some of the nut and seed crunch. Split the bags at the table and serve with some sugar-free ice cream.

These cookies are a treat on their own.

Cinnamon Apple
Upside-Down Pudding

SERVES 4

4 red apples
60g (2 oz) butter
1 teaspoon ground
   cinnamon
pinch ground cloves
pinch ground nutmeg
3 tablespoons agave nectar
Pudding mixture
120g (4oz) fresh ricotta
½ teaspoon vanilla essence
120ml (4fl oz) milk (2% fat)
60g (2oz) butter
2 eggs, separated
1 teaspoon superfine/caster
   sugar
2 tablespoons ground
   almonds
2 tablespoons bakers/self-
   raising flour, sifted
2 tablespoons flaked
   almonds

1. Preheat oven to 160°C (320°F). Peel, core and cut each
   apple into 8 wedges.
2. Melt 60g (2oz) butter in a small pan with the spices and 2
   tablespoons agave nectar. Coat the apple wedges in this and
   place wedges onto a non-stick baking tray. Bake in oven for
   20 minutes until soft and caramelised.
3. Remove from the oven and while still hot place apple wedges
   into a deep ovenproof baking dish (I like to use a glass dish
   for this).
4. Warm the milk and vanilla with the remaining 1 tablespoon of
   agave nectar and 60g (2oz) of butter, melt together and then
   allow it to cool.
5. In a mixer beat the ricotta for 3 minutes until smooth and
   creamy, add the egg yolks and the milk mxture. Then mix in
   the ground almonds and flour combine together.
6. In a separate bowl, whisk the egg whites to a stiff peak with
   the caster sugar. Fold these egg whites into the mixture and
   pour mixture over the caramalised apples, sprinkle the top with
   the flaked almonds.
7. Bake in the oven for 30 minutes until golden and firm to the
   touch.

99

Serve this warm as a great
alternative to apple pie, without the
fat or sugar content.

Citrus & Poppy Seed Cake

SERVES 12

CAKE MIXTURE

2 lemons
3 large oranges
700ml (24fl oz) water
3 tablespoons agave nectar
2 cardamom pods
30g (1oz) butter
3 eggs, lightly beaten
240g (3oz) ground almonds
2 tablespoons poppy seeds
2 tablespoons bakers/self-
    raising flour
2 tablespoons whey protein
    powder
1 teaspoon baking soda/
    bicarbonate of soda

SYRUP

2 tablespoons freshly
    squeezed orange juice
juice of ¼ of a lemon
1 tablespoon agave nectar

1. Peel lemons and oranges, discard rind, and slice fruit approximately ½cm (¼in) thick.
2. Place fruit in a medium-sized saucepan with the water, agave nectar and 2 cardamom pods. Cover with a lid and place on a medium heat to simmer for approximately 2 hours until the fruit is totally cooked and broken down, and has a marmalade-like consistency. Take care not to burn as it will become very sticky as it nears the end of its cooking.
3. Preheat oven to 180°C (360°F).
4. Remove the cardamom pods and discard. Stir in the butter to melt and allow mixture to cool.
5. Place fruit into a mixing bowl and mix in the lightly beaten eggs.
6. Stir in the ground almonds, protein powder, bicarbonate of soda, poppy seeds and the flour. Mix well together. It will be quite loose at this point.
7. Line an 20cm (8in) cake tin with greaseproof paper and a spray of oil. Pour in the cake mixture and bake for 25 minutes until golden and firm to touch.
8. Meanwhile, to make the syrup, warm the lemon and orange juice with the agave.
9. Once cooked, remove the cake from the oven and allow to cool on a cooling wire. Turn it over and place onto your serving plate, brush it with the warm syrup and allow it to soak in.

Peanut Butter & Chocolate Mini Tartlets

MAKES APPROXIMATELY 20 SMALL TARTLETS, 2 PER PORTION

½ packet filo pastry
60g (2oz) butter, melted
1 tablespoon agave nectar
175ml (6fl oz) light cream
½ teaspoon vanilla essence
120g (4oz) dark chocolate
  buttons
  (71% chocolate)
80g (3oz) low-fat crunchy
  peanut butter
1 tablespoon dark cocoa
fresh raspberries or
  strawberries to garnish

1. Preheat oven to 180°C (360°F). Brush a sheet of filo pastry with melted butter and place another sheet of filo on top. Repeat with two other layers. Cut layered filo using a pastry ring to fit the size of small tartlet moulds, approximately 3cm (1in) in diameter. Line the moulds with the filo and some baking parchment discs, then place some rice or beans inside, to act as pastry weights.

2. Blind bake pastry in the oven for 3 minutes, remove from oven and discard the pastry weights and parchment. Return pastry shells to the oven and bake for a further 3 minutes until golden and crisp. Remove from the oven and allow to cool.

3. In a small saucepan, bring the agave and the cream to the boil with the vanilla essence. Place chocolate buttons into a bowl and pour over hot cream mix. Stir together until smooth. Set aside and allow to cool, but do not refrigerate.

4. If chocolate hasn't melted enough microwave it briefly.

5. To make the tartlets, place some peanut butter in the bottom of each one and pipe or spoon the chocolate mixture on the top. Dust with a little dark cocoa and finish with a raspberry or a strawberry.

Peach, Pear & Raspberry Semifreddo

SERVES 4

120g (4oz) canned pears, drained to produce 60ml (2fl oz) syrup
½ punnet fresh raspberries
2 tablespoons cornstarch/ cornflour
2 tablespoons agave nectar
120g (4oz) canned peaches, drained
230ml (8fl oz) milk
175g (6oz) natural yogurt

1. Warm the pear syrup and pour over the fresh raspberries. Place in the fridge to cool.
2. Mix the cornstarch, agave nectar and 2 tablespoons of the milk.
3. Bring remaining milk to the boil and stir in the cornstarch mixture stirring well until it thickens. Remove from the heat, cover and allow to cool.
4. In a blender place the pears and peaches. Drain the syrup from the raspberries and set them aside.
5. Blend the pears and peaches until smooth, then add the cold milk custard mixture and combine together.
6. Add the natural yogurt and mix well.
7. Line a small loaf tin or ramekin dishes with plastic wrap and pour in the mixture.
8. Drop one or two raspberries into each dish and place into the freezer for at least 3 hours to set.
9. Remove from the freezer for 45 minutes before serving.

This is a refreshing light alternative to ice cream.

Not-So-Naughty Chocolate Cake

MAKES ONE LARGE 3-LAYERED CAKE | SERVES 12

300g (10oz) fresh full cream
   ricotta cheese
30g (1oz) unsweetened pure
   cocoa powder
120ml (4fl oz) fresh milk (2% fat)
2 tablespoons agave nectar
60g (2oz) butter
3 large fresh eggs
175g (6oz) bakers/self-raising
   flour
½ teaspoon baking soda/
   bicarbonate of soda
60g (2oz) ground almonds
120ml (4fl oz) cream, lightly
   whisked with 1 teaspoon
   agave nectar
fresh berries or figs, dark
   chocolate shavings and
   confectioners'/icing sugar to
   serve

CHOCOLATE TOPPING
120ml (4fl oz) light cream
2 drops vanilla essence
1 teaspoon agave nectar
120g (4oz) dark chocolate, 71%
   cocoa

1. Preheat oven to 180°C (360°F). In a large mixing bowl or electric kitchen mixer place the ricotta and, using the beater attachment, mix vigorously for 3 minutes until very smooth.
2. Mix the cocoa into a small amount of the milk, then warm it with the remaining milk and agave nectar. Stir in the butter to melt then allow to cool.
3. In a separate bowl, lightly whisk eggs with a fork.
4. Sift the flour, bicarbonate of soda and ground almonds onto a sheet of baking parchment.
5. With the mixer on a medium speed, gradually add the egg to the ricotta then add the milk and butter mixture. Add the almonds and flour mix together and combine. Do not over mix at this point.
6. Grease and line a 20cm (8in) cake tin with baking parchment. Pour mix into tin and bake in oven for 30 minutes—do not open oven during cooking.
7. Invert cake on to a cooling wire rack and allow to cool.
8. Make the chocolate topping. In a small pan, warm the cream, vanilla and agave nectar. Remove from heat and add the chocolate. Stir until mixed and allow to cool. Do not refrigerate.
9. Using a large bread knife, slice the cake into three pieces horizontally. Then spread each layer with some of the chocolate topping, the whisked cream and the fresh fruit. Finally garnish the top with some dark chocolate shavings and a very light dusting of confectioners' sugar. To make chocolate shavings scrape a sharp knife over a bar of (room temperature) dark chocolate or use a vegetable peeler

Blood Sugar: Food to Share

About the Author

With a career spanning almost three decades, Michael Moore is renowned for his work as a chef, author and TV presenter. He has cooked for some of the world's top celebrities and has become a household name on shows such as Fresh, Junior MasterChef and The Biggest Loser and appears on NBC's Today Show and New York's Morning News, reaching an audience of 29 million viewers.

Raised in England, Michael developed a love of cooking at an early age. It was while studying classical cookery at college that he developed his interest in the scientific aspects of food and nutrition that have come to set him apart from his peers today.

Five years ago, personal circumstances changed the trajectory of his career. He was already living with diabetes and for a top chef surrounded by great food, he faced the daily challenge of healthy eating. Then, one day out of the blue, he suffered a major stroke while out to dinner with his family, an event that changed his life forever.

It was this episode that inspired his best selling Blood Sugar cook book series; a collection of beautifully presented and inspiring recipes that break the mould in diabetic cooking.

'Being a diabetic doesn't mean you are stuck in a "gastronomic wilderness". You can enjoy great food that's unexpected and exciting whilst keeping your sugars under control', says Michael.

This healthy eating philosophy underpins the menus at his restaurant O Bar and Dining, located in Sydney's CBD. The food is an unexpected journey of contemporary dining with a healthy spin.

Michael is a committed charity Ambassador and supporter to The National Breast Cancer Foundation, The Sydney Children's Hospital Foundation, Starlight Children's Foundation, St. Vincent's Hospital Foundation and more recently, The Garvan Institute of Medical Reseach, National Stroke Foundation and Diabetes Australia.

Michael currently sits on Tourism Australia's Advisory Board as a culinary ambassador.

With his profile and brand continuing to build internationally as he spreads his message about healthy eating, this global entrepreneur is set to continue to reinvent the dining experience on both sides of the world.

Follow Michael Moore on social media:
Twitter – @michaelmooresyd
Facebook –www.facebook.com/ChefMichaelMoore

Twitter – @obardining
Facebook – www.facebook.com/Obardining
Instagram – @obardining
www.obardining.com.au

Index

First published in 2015 by New Holland Publishers Pty Ltd
London • Sydney • Auckland

www.newhollandpublishers.com

A record of this book is held at the British Library and the National Library of Australia.

ISBN 9781742578507

Managing Director: Fiona Schultz
Project Editor: Jessica McNamara
Designer: Lorena Susak
Production Director: Olga Dementiev
Printer: Toppan Leefung Printing Limited

10 9 8 7 6 5 4 3 2 1

Keep up with New Holland Publishers on Facebook
www.facebook.com/NewHollandPublishers